21st CENTURY
Junior Library

INFOGRAPHICS:
SCARCITY

OUT OF STOCK

T0002422

Econo-Graphics Jr.

Christina Hill

Published in the United States of America by Cherry Lake Publishing Group

Cherry Lake Publishing Group
Ann Arbor, Michigan
www.cherrylakepublishing.com

Reading Adviser: Beth Walker Gambro, MS, Ed., Reading Consultant, Yorkville, IL
Photo Credits: Cover, Page 1: ©Nanzeeba Ibnat/Getty Images; Page 4: ©Ikiry GR/Shutterstock; Page 5: ©Colorlife/Shutterstock, ©keko-ka/ Shutterstock; Page 6: ©Shafin Al Asad Protic/Pixabay; Page 7: ©Viktoria Kurpas/Shutterstock; Page 8: ©Vectorfair/Shutterstock; Page 9: ©the8monkey/Shutterstock; Page 10: ©200 Degrees/Pixabay, ©Lemberg Vector studio/Shutterstock, ©Mind Pixell/Shutterstock, ©OpenClipart-Vectors/Pixabay; Page 13: ©Georgii Red/Shutterstock, ©Nicoleta Ionescu/Shutterstock; Page 14: ©ClassicVector/Shutterstock; Page 16: ©Clker-Free-Vector-Images/Pixabay, ©stux/Pixabay; Page 17: ©kozhedub_nc/Shutterstock; Page 20: ©m.malinika/Shutterstock; Page 21: ©Evgeniya Cherevatenko/Shutterstock; Page 22: ©Gilberto Rodrigues/Pixabay, ©JJuni/Pixabay, ©OpenClipart-Vectors/Pixabay, ©Werner Moser/Pixabay

Cherry Lake Press is an imprint of Cherry Lake Publishing Group.

Library of Congress Cataloging-in-Publication Data
Names: Hill, Christina, author.
Title: Infographics. Scarcity / Christina Hill.
Other titles: Scarcity
Description: Ann Arbor, Michigan : Cherry Lake Publishing, [2023] | Series: Econo-graphics Jr. | Includes bibliographical references and index. | Audience: Grades 2-3 | Summary: "Why is it important to understand scarcity? In the Econo-Graphics Jr. series, young readers will examine economy-related issues from many angles, all portrayed through visual elements. Income, budgeting, investing, supply and demand, global markets, inflation, and more are covered. Each book highlights pandemic-era impacts as well. Created with developing readers in mind, charts, graphs, maps, and infographics provide key content in an engaging and accessible way. Books include an activity, glossary, index, suggested reading and websites, and a bibliography"— Provided by publisher.
Identifiers: LCCN 2022037922 | ISBN 9781668919255 (hardcover) | ISBN 9781668920275 (paperback) | ISBN 9781668921609 (ebook) | ISBN 9781668922934 (pdf)
Subjects: LCSH: Supply and demand—Juvenile literature. | Scarcity—Juvenile literature.
Classification: LCC HB801 .H5223 2023 | DDC 331.12—dc23/eng/20220907
LC record available at https://lccn.loc.gov/2022037922
Cherry Lake Publishing Group would like to acknowledge the work of the Partnership for 21st Century Learning, a network of Battelle for Kids. Please visit http://www.battelleforkids.org/networks/p21 for more information.

Printed in the United States of America
Corporate Graphics

Before embracing a career as an author, **Christina Hill** received a bachelor's degree in English from the University of California, Irvine, and a graduate degree in literature from California State University, Long Beach. When she is not writing about various subjects from sports to economics, Christina can be found hiking, mastering yoga handstands, or curled up with a classic novel. Christina lives in sunny Southern California with her husband, two sons, and beloved dog, Pepper Riley.

CONTENTS

WHAT IS SCARCITY?

When something is scarce, it has a limit. **Scarcity** is a problem in the economy. It happens when **resources** are limited, but people have unlimited wants. Scarcity means that everyone must make important choices.

Scarcity Affects Everyone

Individuals

All people have limited time and money. A person can work more to make more money. But they are giving their time to do so.

Businesses

Businesses must make money to stay open. Before they can make money, they must pay for things. These things include workers, supplies, and materials.

Relative Scarcity Example

Relative scarcity is when a resource supply is limited but the resource is still in demand.

In 2021, computer microchips were scarce. The COVID-19 pandemic made it take more time to make microchips. At the same time, the demand for electronics went up.

Estimated Number of Cars Taken Out of Production Due to Lack of Microchips

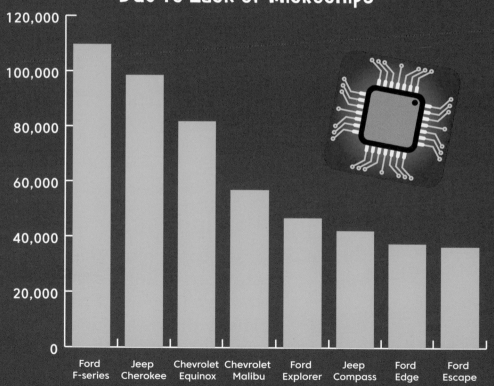

120,000	
100,000	
80,000	
60,000	
40,000	
20,000	
0	

Ford F-series · Jeep Cherokee · Chevrolet Equinox · Chevrolet Malibu · Ford Explorer · Jeep Compass · Ford Edge · Ford Escape

2021, Statista

Absolute Scarcity

Absolute scarcity happens when a resource is limited. Humans can't do anything to increase the amount. Demand doesn't matter.

Time is an example of absolute scarcity.

60 minutes in an hour

24 hours in a day

7 days in a week

12 months in a year

10 years in a decade

LIMITED RESOURCES

Nearly all resources are limited. A resource must meet our wants and needs. Time, money, and labor are resources. They are used to make goods and services. Water, trees, oil, plants, and rocks are natural resources.

The Three Types of Resources

Natural Resources

Things found in nature that are used by humans

water

oil

stone and
minerals

animals

coal

The Three Types of Resources

Human Resources

Any labor done by people to make goods and services for sale

doctors   construction workers   chefs   teachers   artists

Capital Resources

Machines and tools used to make goods and services

farming equipment

computers

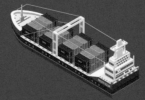

airplanes   ships   forklifts

Renewable and Nonrenewable Resources
All resources are limited, but some things can be renewed!
Other things are nonrenewable.

RENEWABLE	NONRENEWABLE
Resources that can be renewed	Resources that can be used up and are not easy to renew

 Biomass: trees, crops, and animal waste

 Coal: rocks burned for fuel

Geothermal: heat energy from inside the planet

Natural Gas: gas used for energy

 Hydropower: moving water used for energy

 Oil: liquid found deep underground that is used for fuel

Solar: energy from the Sun

Propane: gas used in grills and machines for energy

Wind: energy from moving air

Uranium: special rock used for nuclear power

UNLIMITED WANTS

Our world is full of limited resources. But we have unlimited wants. So how do these two things balance? People must make choices. Every choice has an **opportunity cost**. It's what you give up when you choose something else.

Opportunity Cost in Business

Business owners think about opportunity costs when they make decisions.

For example, a construction company uses wood to build houses. The project manager has two wood suppliers she likes.

Choosing the cheaper supplier would save money. But she will have to wait a month for the wood to ship from another country.

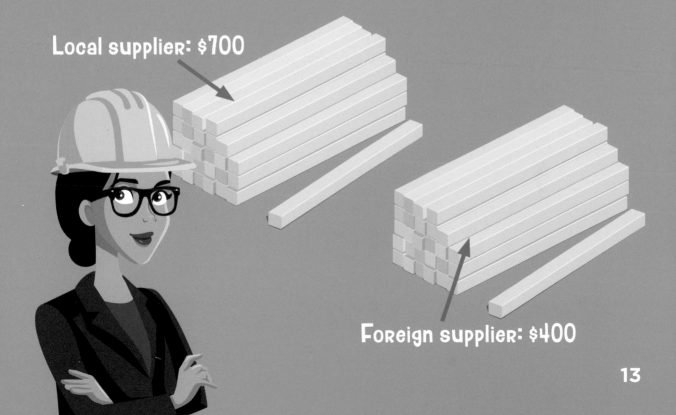

Local supplier: $700

Foreign supplier: $400

Opportunity Cost in Business

If the project manager chooses the local supplier, she can pick up wood today. Then her team can start building right away.

The project manager chooses the local supplier. What is her opportunity cost? It's the money she could have saved by using the cheaper lumber.

EXTREME SCARCITY

The world population keeps growing over time. But nonrenewable resources are limited. A healthy economy is one with balance. It balances unlimited wants with limited resources. But not everyone gets the same amount of resources.

In some places resources are extremely scarce. This leads to people living in **poverty**. Their choices are limited to basic needs. These include food, water, clothing, and shelter.

Water Scarcity

Water is everywhere! It covers 70% of our planet.

2.5% is freshwater

97.5% is saltwater

North Africa: LEAST access to renewable freshwater per person

South America: MOST access to renewable freshwater per person

12%
is used by industry

16%
is used by households and services

72%
of all water is used by agriculture

Water use is growing at more than twice the rate of population in the last 100 years.

Around 2.3 billion people live in countries with water scarcity.

2021, UN-Water

Top Regions with Food Scarcity (2020)

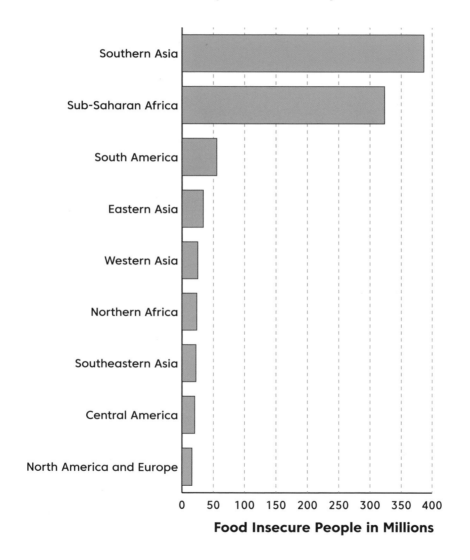

Food Insecure People in Millions

2022, Statista

GLOBAL EFFORTS

Climate change has affected nearly all natural resources. The world is working together to make plans for scarcity issues. These plans deal with hunger, poverty, and clean water. The plans will help resources last for future generations.

Climate Change and Resources

2021 was the sixth-hottest year on record for the planet.

Warm temperatures are causing a rise in sea levels. This means there is less land to live on. By 2100, scientists think more than 150 million people will need to move. This is because their homes will be underwater.

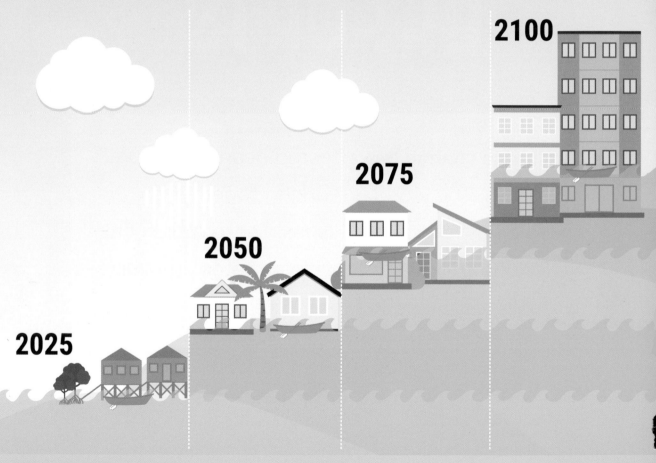

2100

2075

2050

2025

Fast Facts

- There is enough food to feed everyone in the world. Organizations are working to send food to places it is scarce.

- Worldwide, the number of people without enough food has dropped. It dropped from 15% in 2000–2004 to 8.9% in 2019.

2021, Food and Agriculture Organization of the United Nations

ACTIVITY
What's the Opportunity Cost?

Track five choices you must make in one day. These could be what to wear or how to spend your time. Record the opportunity cost for each decision.

Review the sample chart below. Then choose one of your choices and fill out the empty chart.

Today's Choice	Now		Later	
Buying a $5 fruit smoothie	Spending $5 another way today		Saving the $5 for later use	

Today's Choice	Now		Later	

LEARN MORE

Books

The Economics Book: Big Ideas Simply Explained. New York: DK Publishing, 2018.

Redling, Dylin, and Allison Tom. *Investing for Kids: How to Save, Invest, and Grow Money*. Emeryville, CA: Rockridge Press, 2020.

Websites

Britannica Kids: Natural Resource
https://kids.britannica.com/kids/article/natural-resource/399553

PBS Learning Media: Think Garden: Buying Local
https://tpt.pbslearningmedia.org/resource/2f19600e-2c75-4ce2-93a1-c40cc1424f48/think-garden-buying-local

Bibliography

Stigler, G. J., and Baumol, William J. *"Price system."* Encyclopedia Britannica, June 6, 2011. https://www.britannica.com/topic/price-system

The Editors of Encyclopedia Britannica. *"Opportunity Cost."* Encyclopedia Britannica. August 27, 2019. https://www.britannica.com/topic/opportunity-cost

Maunz, Shay. *"Waste Not."* April 10, 2019. https://www.timeforkids.com/g56/waste-not-2/?rl=en-880

GLOSSARY

climate change (KLY-muht CHAYNJ) the shifts of Earth's temperatures and weather patterns over time

demand (dih-MAND) desire to purchase goods and services

nonrenewable (NAHN-rih-NOO-uh-buhl) unable to be restored or replaced

opportunity cost (ah-puhr-TOO-nuh-tee KAHST) benefit someone gives up when they choose something else

poverty (PAH-vuhr-tee) the state of being poor

renewed (rih-NOOD) restored or replaced

resources (REE-sohrs-ez) things a country has and can use to increase its wealth

scarcity (SKAYR-suh-tee) limited or small supply; not enough

supply (suh-PLY) amount of something available to be used

INDEX